Eastern Customs of the Bible:

The Teachings of Bishop K. C. Pillai

Jeanie Strand Chilton

Order this book online at www.trafford.com
or email orders@trafford.com

Most Trafford titles are also available at major online book retailers.

Printed in Victoria, BC, Canada.

ISBN: 978-1-4251-2163-1 (Soft)

*We at Trafford believe that it is the responsibility of us all, as both individuals
and corporations, to make choices that are environmentally and socially sound.
You, in turn, are supporting this responsible conduct each time you purchase a
Trafford book, or make use of our publishing services. To find out how you are
helping, please visit www.trafford.com/responsiblepublishing.html*

*Our mission is to efficiently provide the world's finest, most comprehensive
book publishing service, enabling every author to experience success.
To find out how to publish your book, your way, and have it available
worldwide, visit us online at www.trafford.com*

Trafford rev. 11/16/2009

Trafford
PUBLISHING® www.trafford.com

North America & international
toll-free: 1 888 232 4444 (USA & Canada)
phone: 250 383 6864 ♦ fax: 812 355 4082 ♦ email: info@trafford.com

In loving memory of
Oliver T. Strand, Jr.
1919-1988

Husband, father, pastor,
and all-around good guy.

ACKNOWLEDGEMENTS

My special thanks and sincere appreciation to
Dolores (Lorie) Segaard and Silvie Hardee for their valuable
contribution to the proofreading of this manuscript.

CONTENTS

Acknowledgements   vii
Preface   xi
Introduction   xv
Chapter 1   WHEN WAS CHRIST BORN?   1
Chapter 2   WHAT DO THE PLANTS KNOW?   3
Chapter 3   FIVE TREES   7
Chapter 4   WIDOWS IN THE BIBLE   9
Chapter 5   THE SAMARITAN WOMAN   13
Chapter 6   THE DELICATE VESSELS   17
Chapter 7   SHEEP AND SHEPHERDS   23
Chapter 8   SEALED BY THE SPIRIT   29
Chapter 9   SACKCLOTH, ASHES AND DUST   33
Chapter 10   RAHAB THE "HARLOT"   37
Chapter 11   PUNISHMENT BY LAW   41
Chapter 12   OUR DAILY BREAD   45
Chapter 13   MORE CULTURE CLASHES   49
Chapter 14   MEET ME AT THE GATE   53
Chapter 15   LET'S BE SALTED   55
Chapter 16   JUST AND UNJUST STEWARDS   59
Chapter 17   HOW THEY GOT MARRIED   63
Chapter 18   THE DINNER THAT FAILED   67
Chapter 19   EAGLES   71
Chapter 20   HOW TO DIE WELL   77
Epilogue   81
Appendix A   Eastern Customs Of The Bible   85
Appendix B   Cursing And Blessing - An Abstract Concept   87

PREFACE

God gave His Word in words easy to understand. He chose words in common use among His people when His Word was originally given. He spoke to them in terms they could understand – not only in their language, but also according to their customs and manners – so they could fulfill His will. The customs and manners found in the Bible are those of the Eastern or Oriental world. They are quite different from those in the Western or Occidental world. Because the Bible is an Eastern book, it is essential to study and understand the customs and manners of the Eastern people who originally heard it.

Many of the customs and manners of the Bible have survived to this century in India. Because India has remained an isolated country for thousands of years, the customs and manners of the people have been well preserved. Many of these customs and manners have continued until this day from the times the original revelation was given.

Dr. Bishop K. C. Pillai (1900-1970) was a Bishop-at-large of the Indian Orthodox Church, Antiochean Succession, Madras, India. He spent the last twenty years of his life in the United States of America on a special mission to acquaint Christians with the Orientalisms of the Bible. His teachings, books, and work with believers provide a unique contribution in clarifying difficult Scriptural passages via an understanding of the Eastern customs and manners in the Bible. Here's an example:

Luke 11:11

If a son shall ask bread of any of you that is a father, will
he give him a stone?
"Bread in the East is not like what you are familiar with
in the western world. Each piece is round and flat, about
the size of a dinner plate. It is very thin and is cooked
on both sides. . . When the bread is done it is placed
on a stone which is about the same size as the bread.
Ordinarily there would be several Chappatis as we call
the bread, in one stack. Then another stone would be
placed on top to protect the bread. The women use
ghee, which is like butter, in cooking the bread. Over a
period of time the stones soak up the ghee and actually
take on the appearance of the bread. . . Obviously, any
Eastern father would know the difference between the
stone and the bread, and he would never give the stone
when his son has asked for bread." [1]

I am nearly 60 years of age. But I discovered Dr. Pillai's work
just a year ago. His discovery was made possible by a far more
startling and personal discovery involving my long lost Aunt
Jeanie May, the author of this text. My Dad told me stories of
his little sister all of his life. They separated when their parents
divorced and Dad left home at age 16. Dad looked for her all his
life, and on his deathbed, in August 1998, among his last words
was the expression of regret that he had never found Jeanie May.
"It would have been so nice to have seen her again."

More than eight years passed, and the Lord made a miraculous
connection. Through a genealogical web search by a mother
helping her Eagle-seeking Boy Scout son, an electronic message-
in-a-bottle seeking "Lees among the Younts," dropped into the
web-ocean by my wife, was found. The mother was Dorothy,
and the son was Jacob. The message in the bottle requested

---

1   Information on Bishop Pillai by Micheal Cortright. http://
www.cortright.org/key6.htm

information on Dorothy's grandmother, Helen Lee Yount. And Dorothy's mother . . . is *Jeanie May.* Aunt Jeanie May still lives in Denton, Texas, near Dorothy. And why do I tell this story in the midst of a Preface on Bishop Pillai?

Because it was *Jeanie May* who introduced me to Bishop Pillai. But far more profound is this, known by few: it was Jeanie May who saw the wisdom in his lectures, and secured his permission, and painstakingly transcribed his spoken words to paper.

The first volume Aunt Jeanie compiled for Dr. Pillai was *Light Through an Eastern Window,* his first work, published in 1963. Search as you might, you will not find Jeanie's name anywhere in the book. Nor any recognition or acknowledgement. Acknowledgment of a woman's academic work was uncommon in 1963. Moreover, the Bishop might have been embarrassed to admit that a woman had actually written his teachings down for him. They also produced two volumes of *Orientalisms of the Bible.* Jeanie May wrote me an email about Bishop Pillai in late 2006, in which she said,

> "I double-checked everything I wrote down according to Scripture, because I didn't want to be found writing something was contrary to the Bible. This period of learning and research and writing was a great period of personal and spiritual growth."

And so I am thankful to Bishop Pillai for his wisdom and insight. But I am far more thankful to the Lord that he allowed me to know my Dad's little sister, and her family. I can do nothing but praise the Lord for bringing both Jeanie May and Billy Yount out of the darkness of unbelief and broken family to a bright faith in Jesus Christ. And now, because of her, I can learn from the good Bishop, first because she translated that which was spoken to a form I can now hold in my hands. And second, because I know of him and his ministry only because I know her. And that is a double blessing, indeed.

May you gain rich blessings as well from this story of discovery and insight, from my Aunt Jeanie May's own hand.

William "Rick" Yount
Created to Learn (1996), *Called to Teach* (1999), *Called to Reach* (2007) B&H Publishers: Nashville
October 2007

INTRODUCTION

The Bible is a book with which I have been fascinated all my life, but never so much as after I met the Ft. Rev. Bishop K. C. Pillai of the Indian Orthodox Church.

It was a chilly night in Ohio in 1961 when I first heard the Bishop speak. It was a life-changing experience. His simple, logical explanations of Bible verses left everyone filled with awe and excitement.

"These teachings must be written down," I commented to the group afterwards. "If you'll excuse my saying so, Bishop, you aren't getting any younger, and you can only teach a small group of people at a time."

"I am supporting a group of seminary students in India just now, and I must keep asking for offerings to meet my commitment to them. Also, I would need an editor to help with my English since my first language is Hindi. I also have Sanskrit. So you see, I would need a writer for the English part."

I raised my hand. "I am a writer," I said. "I will come wherever you are teaching and take down what you say, then you can go over it afterward. Just tell me where you are going next and I will be there."

As I recall, he looked a little doubtful at the time, but maybe he figured it wouldn't hurt to see how this scheme turned out. And I hadn't asked him for any money.

The task of understanding each other became more than simple language "snafus." The Bishop's idea of a woman's place in the scheme of things kept coming up. I tried not to say anything about it, because I wanted to focus on the task of getting the valuable insights written and produced.

For instance, he let me know that I was not to ever be in a room with him alone. One time he was staying with a family nearby and I had a section written which I was not too sure about and wanted him to look it over. When I got there, the lady of the house was not there. "Where is Mrs. B?" I asked.

"Oh, she went to get some groceries," he replied.

My daughter, Dorothy, was a toddler and I was carrying her on my hip, so we weren't exactly alone. But, the Bishop suddenly got that horrified look people get when they know that a faux pas has been committed. He seemed very uncomfortable, so I didn't wait for him to read the pages I had brought, picking them up at a later time.

Mrs. B told me that if the Bishop should ask to borrow money, that we should just kiss it goodbye. "He believes that if a Holy Man asks for anything you ought to just give it to him. Just warning you," she said.

We heard nothing about this for many months, but one day a letter came in the mail from the Bishop. He wanted to borrow $100. I told my husband what Mrs. B had said; we should look at it as a contribution, I explained. We had a "tithe" account and took the money out of that and forgot about it.

Several years later, when my husband had resigned his position at Wright-Patterson Air Force Base and enrolled in Seminary, we heard from the Bishop again. He sent us a check for $100 and seemed quite "put out" that we hadn't informed him of our new situation.

Light Through an Eastern Window was published by Speller and Son of New York in 1963, followed by paperback editions beginning in 1985. The last I heard, it was still available through Amazon.com.

Through the years, many people have sent me additional teachings from the Bishop's visits to their part of the country. I have been in touch with a nun from California who said she drove the Bishop from one appearance to another just so she could hear more of his teachings. *The Way* magazine (New Knoxville, Ohio) printed a series of his teachings and I have used some of them.

However, I have used my own discretion as to whether something should be included in this volume. The Bishop often did not realize whether something which he wished to share was understandable to the Western mind. Some one did a little book on the Psalms virtually verbatim as to his remarks, and many verses were followed by a comment, "That is so typical of Eastern thought." Maybe so, but if it was no big mystery to the Western mind, I omitted it.

I was just a young mother when I did *Light Through an Eastern Window* for the Bishop. I am now 82 years old, and a grandmother eight times over. I cannot end my days without sharing additional enlightening and encouraging understandings of the Bible that the Bishop brought to us. At one time I foolishly thought that the book would magically circulate throughout the Christian work, making the Bible abundantly clear to everyone. All I know is, every time I loaned out a copy, I never got it back, because they loaned it to someone else, who in turn --- you get the idea.

In 1970, when my husband was just getting ready to graduate from Seminary, the Bishop died. I was sitting at the copy desk at the Springfield Sun newspaper in Springfield, Ohio, when a call came in from a funeral parlor. I was barely able to take down the information: this was MY Bishop they were talking about.

We had no idea the Bishop was living so close by. Apparently, he had been living in a nursing home in Fairborn, at the edge of Wright-Patterson Air Force Base. When we entered the viewing room, I could scarcely believe my eyes. The Bishop was laid out in all his clerical robes, a shepherd's crook in the casket with him, a miter on his head and his folded hands displaying the jewels of his office.

There had never been an occasion for me to see him in any clothing except his severe black suit, with the clerical shirt and white collar. We certainly didn't appreciate his high standing when he walked among us, displaying a humility, which the rest of us could well have copied. (One Christian attribute, which he lacked, was his attitude toward the British. He mentioned that when he got to England to attend Seminary, he met many elderly people who have sacrificed to support missionaries in India, little realizing that their money was going to a chaplain who ran a school for the British children, married and buried the flock and lived high on the hog with at least five servants each. None of the money went to reach the natives of India. As I said in the former book, the Bishop himself was won to Christ through a native preacher from a neighboring town.)

One last remnant of his attitude toward women: he wouldn't bring himself to say in the front of the *Light Through an Eastern Window* that I had written the book for him. He was too proud, I think, to let that be known. He did thank me for "assisting him with the manuscript." Maybe this was before the days when people would put their name on a book as the author and then add "with" to indicate who actually did the writing. I would have been happy with an "as told to."

Jeanie Strand Chilton
Denton, Texas, 2008

Chapter 1

WHEN WAS CHRIST BORN?

"Bishop," someone said once when we had gathered in a friend's home, "I read someplace that December 25 was not the actual date of the birth of Christ. Would you say that we celebrate it on the wrong day?"

He began, "My understanding of how we came to celebrate the birth of Christ in December comes from a tradition which I heard about while in England. It is said that when Constantine became a Christian, he became so enthusiastic that he declared his whole realm to be Christian.

"Of course, we do not become a Christian through someone's statement that we are, and it was not long before the formerly pagan people complained that they missed their favorite holiday. It was called "Childmas" (a mass for a child god). So Constantine decreed that they could celebrate the holiday, but to call it Christmas (a mass for Christ).

"Personally, I believe that Christ came during a time when the weather was warm, perhaps August or September, because the shepherds were out in the open with their sheep.

"You may wonder why none of the early writers made it his business to preserve the exact time of Christ's advent, so that we could have the right date. I believe it is because the Eastern people do not pay much attention to birthdays. They believe that since everyone gets born, it's nothing remarkable. They think that how and when a man dies is the important thing. By that time the people know whether he has lived a good life. If he has, they will honor him on the day that he died. In my country they honor Mahatma Gandhi on the day that he passed away."

"Don't they celebrate birthdays at all?" we asked.

"Yes, the people know their birthday dates within their own families. The way they celebrate is to give gifts to others, in gratitude to God for their lives."

"I can't see that catching on here," someone said.

After the laughter had quieted, he continued, "Do you remember in Isaiah 55:1, which says, 'Ho, every one that thirsteth, come ye to the waters, and he that hath no money; come ye and buy, and eat; yea, come, buy wine and milk without money and without price.'?"

"Doesn't that mean that salvation is free to us, but was paid for by Christ?" someone asked.

"Very good. But beside that, this is the cry of a man who is celebrating his birthday by offering water, milk or wine to those passing by. (Don't forget water is precious in a desert area.) This man has brought something of this kind, likely in a goatskin and is standing out on the street inviting others to share in the blessing.

"This is a wonderful verse which is, as you already understood, a foreshadowing of our salvation. God bought it for us. We receive salvation free of charge; it was paid for by another. And what a terrible price He paid! We can scarcely celebrate the birth of our Lord without being reminded that He came to redeem us, that the world through Him might be saved.

"This is why it is not so important that we know exactly when Christ was born; the important thing is that he was born into the world to give us eternal life. We should all be sure that Jesus, the Son of God, has been made Lord of our lives."

Chapter 2

WHAT DO THE PLANTS KNOW?

"In Eastern thought, the people believe that plants know what they are doing," the Bishop once began. As was the case so many times when I heard him speaking, my inner response was "*What does that mean?*"

"Their reasoning is that people are responsible if they put forth bitter fruit and thorns, therefore the plants know these things also. Otherwise, how would they know what way they should grow?

"For instance, the mustard seed. This seed knows it's like a speck of dust, but it has faith that will grow up to be a big bush where birds will roost. Notice that the Scripture says to focus on the faith of the mustard seed, not on the size, as some versions have added."

I was wondering, what's the difference? He continued, "The people are so sure that the plants know what they are doing that they will not associate with any plants which have bitter fruit or thorns, in case they might become that way themselves. They believe that we are known by the company we keep, so they stay away from "bad" plants.

"This is why it is so interesting that Zacchaeus climbed the sycamore tree to get high enough to see Jesus. This tree has bitter fruit, but Zacchaeus did not care. It was more important for him to see Jesus than to worry about what people would think. I believe someone could make a sermon out of that!"

Ezekiel 13:18-23 speaks against women who use trees and plants for occult purposes. These women made pillows which they claimed had special pieces of alleged sacred roots from Tibet or the Himalayas. They put little straps on each side of the pillow so that they could be tied under the armpits or in front of the elbow.

The Bishop said that the women who do these things are possessed of familiar spirits, practicing the pretended art of divination. The pillows are only a few of the various articles used as fetishes or amulets, to deceive and win the people from the true God.

These women are wild tribes-women who have become specialists in pillow-making. The pillows are about two inches square and a half-inch thick, covered with linen. The women come to the people and tell them about their physical malady and predict their future.

When the people are impressed with this occult knowledge, the women suggest that the pillows should be purchased from them so they can be delivered from their sickness. Only the poorest people tend to believe these things, so the payment mentioned in this passage is handfuls of barley and pieces of bread.

The Bishop said that when he was a young pastor, some people came to his door asking if he would come pray for their son. When he arrived at the home, the boy had one of these pillows tied to his arm.

"What is this?" Pillai demanded, pointing to the pillow.

The parents admitted they had bought the pillow from a tribal woman who had promised it would make the boy well.

"And has it made him well?" Pillai asked.

"No; he is worse," they answered. "That is why we came for you: we have heard that your God is powerful."

"Indeed my God is powerful, and He will not share His glory with anyone. I will pray to my God, but first you must remove the pillow, so that nobody can claim that it was responsible for his being made well."

Verse 20 of Isaiah 13 adds "Behold, I am against your pillows, wherewith ye there hunt the souls to make them fly, and I will tear them from your arms, and will let the souls go, even the souls that ye hunt to make them fly." He said "fly" means "to go from place to place."

Many people today believe in healing, but we should discern between the healing which comes from God and that which comes from an occult source. God can work miracles in answer to the prayers of believers, but we must be aware that Satan tries to produce a counterfeit for each of them. Such items as "sacred" wood, amulets, pillows with herbs inside, are all suspect.

Chapter 3

FIVE TREES

Bishop Pillai said, "God must have been partial to trees, because they are mentioned in the Bible from Genesis to Revelation. For instance, there is the palm tree, mentioned in Proverbs 92:12: 'the righteous shall flourish like the palm tree.' How does the palm tree flourish? It stands head and shoulders above the other trees; it provides a home for the eagles (a holy bird, they believe), and every part of the tree is usable for such products as medicine, ink, pillars in the temple, etc." [See *Light Through an Eastern Window* for more details on the palm tree.]

According to this same verse, the righteous shall grow 'like a cedar in Lebanon'. This symbolizes power, prosperity and longevity.

The olive tree is symbolic of the nation of Israel, Hosea 14:26: "The people (of Israel) will be like spreading branches, they will be like the beautiful olive tree." Olive trees live to be very old; the wood is very hard, and the fruit yields olive oil, which is symbolic of the Holy Spirit.

Olive trees are often mentioned in the Bible. One such reference is found in Psalm 128:3: "Thy children [shall be] like olive plants round about thy table." This refers to the fact that this tree produces for about 50 years, and then stops. But in its old age, little plants grow all around it, holding it up and producing fruit. Easterners see this as symbolic of children supporting their

7

parents in old age; if they were not to do this, they would be thought of as infidels.

Almond tree – Ecclesiastes 12:5: Remember your creator in the days of your youth, for your old age is coming. When...not much enjoyment in life...become frail, lose your eyesight, etc., Verse Five, the almond tree will be flowering.

Fig trees are also thought to be sacred, a symbol of prosperity. Besides that, its shadow is beautiful. Mothers working in the fields will place their babies under a fig tree for safekeeping, believing the tree will provide shade and safety for the infant.

In John I: 47-50, Jesus saw Nathanael coming toward him and says, "Behold an Israelite indeed, in whom there is no guile." Nathanael says, "How do you know me?" And Jesus said, "Before Philip called you, while you were under the fig tree, I saw you." This means that Jesus knew him since he was a child.

The Bishop said that of all the fruits of the East, the sweetest fruit grows on the shittim tree. Shittim trees were mentioned in Isaiah as one of those which would be planted by God in the wilderness, along with cedar, myrtle, oil tree, fir, pine, and box tree. (Isaiah 41:19) The shittim tree also has fragrant wood. It was selected by God to make the ark of the covenant to put in the tabernacle, Exodus 25:10, as well as the staves of the ark; these were then overlaid with gold.

Later, when the Israelites made the tabernacle, the people were again directed to use this pleasant-smelling wood for its standing members, pillars and the altar of burnt offering. If God has a favorite tree among all of those which He created, the shittim, (also called shittah) with its sweet fruit and fragrant wood, must have been the one.

Chapter 4

WIDOWS IN THE BIBLE

If a widow had a son old enough to manage things for her, she would be fortunate and well-cared for. Even more distant relatives would buy into the woman and her property, as we find in the book of Ruth, where Boaz became her kinsman-redeemer.

Ruth's first marriage was arranged by Naomi, her mother-in-law. Her second one was a process because it included the family property. Naomi has no more sons to offer Ruth, so now they are tracing down other family members. Boaz is close, but there is another one who is closer.

Ruth 4 gives the details of how this is settled, and Boaz declares he has done this "in order to maintain the name of the dead with his property so that his name will not disappear from among his family, or from the town records." Genealogies are very important in the Israelite thinking because they are all hoping that the Messiah will be in their family line.

But what would happen if there were no relatives at all to handle this woman's estate? This is what the Bible calls being a "widow indeed", I Timothy 5:5. The priest in the synagogue would then appoint somebody to be a steward over her property.

This unfortunately gave the scribes the opportunity to steal from the widows. Jesus spoke of this in Mark 12:38 and in Luke 20:46. Beware of the teachers of the law, he said, they like to walk around in flowing robes and be greeted in the marketplaces... they devour widows' houses and for a show make lengthy prayers.

Jesus meant that the greedy Scribes would go into the temple and make long prayers, hoping to obtain the position of steward for the widow. It would then be easy for them to sign over the property to themselves, saying to the widow, "I have paid all the bills now, and don't worry, I will take care of you. You can work in the kitchen at my house."

Deuteronomy 25:5-10 talks about the Levirate marriage. If brothers are living together and one of them dies without a son, his widow must not marry outside the family. Her husband's brother shall take her and marry her and fulfill the duty of a brother-in-law to her. The first son she bears shall carry on the name of the dead brother so his name shall not be blotted out from Israel.

What if he doesn't want to? If a man does not want to marry his brother's wife, she shall go to the elders of the town gate and say, "My husband's brother refuses to carry on his brother's name in Israel. He will not fulfill the duty of a brother-in-law to me."

Then the elders of the town shall summon him and talk to him. If he persists in saying, "I do not want to marry her," the brother-in-law's widow shall go up to him in the presence of the elders, take off one of his sandals, spit in his face, and say, "This is what is done to the man who will not build up his brother's family line. That man's line shall be known in Israel as The Family of the Unsandaled." (Spitting is a curse.)

In Genesis 38:6 and following, Judah had married and had three sons. He had arranged a marriage between the eldest son and Tamar. This son died and Judah gave Tamar to Onan, the second son. Whenever they were together, he spilled his semen on the ground, because he knew the child would not be considered his. It would be counted as his brother's son for purposes of inheritance. He also died.

There was still Selah, the third son to be considered but he was too young, so Judah told Tamar to go back to her father's house and live there as a widow until Selah grew up. Judah thought,

"Maybe Selah will die like his brothers, and I won't have to think about this any more."

Now comes a long story about how Selah grew up and Tamar was forgotten, how she tricked Judah into fathering twin sons Perez and Zerah. The family line of Perez is found in the closing verses of the book of Ruth 4:18-22. Ruth and Boaz's son was named Obed, who was the father of Jesse, who was the father of King David.

Mary, mother of Jesus, must have been a widow by the time he was crucified, because he put her in the care of John.

Chapter 5

THE SAMARITAN WOMAN

"Now the Samaritan woman was a sinner; she had been divorced five times..." the speaker said.

My daughter and I turned and gave each other one of those "here-we-go-again" looks. This poor woman, whose name is not given in the Scripture, was having her reputation sullied again by Western thought.

Why do we insist on thinking she is a sinful woman? It is because of one phrase which Easterners understand, but which we in our ignorance imagine to be another matter. It's the verse where Jesus is telling the woman about her life. He says, John 4:18, "For Thou hast had five husbands, and he whom thou now hast is not thy husband..."

Right away we say to ourselves, "Aha! She is living in sin with this man."

No, when Jesus said to her, "You have had five husbands," this means she has been widowed five times. Many commentaries say she was divorced, but it doesn't say that.

If a woman were widowed, she would have been passed along to another brother in the family, along with her property. This is explained in Deuteronomy 25:6-7. "...and the man you now have is not your husband." This means they ran out of relatives, so a steward has her property. According to the customs of that time, women did not own property, since most of them were illiterate and would not have been able to manage it.

This could easily be the reason that the Samaritan woman was going to the well: to draw water for use in the steward's kitchen. When I was in Israel, I was talking to some Arab Christians, and asked them about the idea we find in some of our commentaries that further proof that the woman was a sinner was the TIME that she came to the well. It has been said that the "good" women came in the morning, but this lady was ostracized and had to go alone.

The Arab Christians said, "Our women go to the well whenever they need water. If she were, say, a prostitute, she would not have been permitted to use the well at all."

We also do not understand that it was considered proper for Jesus to speak to her to ask for water, since water is life in that part of the world. The surprise, to her, was that he kept on talking to her, since Jews and Samaritans didn't converse; and then he finally got to the instruction, "Go, call thy husband."

You see, nobody was permitted to instruct a woman on spiritual matters without the permission of her husband. Saying "Go, call thy husband," was the signal to her that he was a Rabbi and was prepared to impart spiritual truth to her. Obviously, he already knew that she had no husband, "thou hast well said…" but he was obliged to follow the custom and mention the possibility of a husband who would have to give permission.

When Jesus was confronted with a sinner, he told them to "go and sin no more". He did not accuse this woman. Also, when she went into town to tell the people, they believed her, since the righteous do not listen to sinners.

The Bishop also told us that Samaria was the only Mid-Eastern area where the people observed the custom of going though an engagement period before marriage; all the rest of the marriages tended to be arranged by a matchmaker or family member. So, either way, this woman was probably NOT a sinner as we have been taught.

Later in the same passage, we find these significant words, "She left her waterpot…" This means little to us, but an Easterner would be horrified to read these words. They believed that their household gods dwelled in their waterpots, and to leave one behind would be unthinkable. This shows what a profound effect the experience had upon her, that she would leave her waterpot behind.

I have spent a lot of time through the years defending this woman's reputation, and believe me, it is difficult when so many experts have made up their minds. However, the point to this whole portion in the Gospel of John is the wonderful truths which Jesus was imparting to the Samaritan lady. "God is Spirit," he said to her (not "a" Spirit according to the Greek text.) "and we must worship Him in Spirit and in Truth." Let's get our minds off whether this person was sinful and look at the message!

Chapter 6

THE DELICATE VESSELS

Bishop Pillai pointed out several places in the Scriptures which have meanings hidden to us because we do not know the customs of the time.

At one time the women saved their tears in a bottle. This reference is found in Psalm 56:8, "Thou tellest my wanderings: put thou my tears into thy bottle: are they not in thy book?"

Many times when women were subjugated they had to cry in secret. But they wanted God to see how much they had suffered, so they thought if they would save their tears in a bottle, it could be buried with them.

If they had cried out of anger, those tears were not saved. It was only the righteous tears which were saved. But this verse says that God keeps His records in a book. This makes it clear that we shouldn't make up practices which we *think* will please God. His plan is to put it all in a book, so the idea of saving tears is not acceptable to Him.

One of the great satisfactions of my life has been finding proof elsewhere that what the Bishop had taught us was, in fact, shared by others. On my trip to Israel (in 1988) our tour had a speaker from an archaeological group who told of having unearthed tear bottles. Then he referenced Luke 7:37-38, where a woman came into the house where Jesus was eating, bringing an alabaster box of ointment, "...and began to wash his feet with tears, wiping them with her hair."

The archaeologist explained that the woman had brought her tear bottle to wash Jesus' feet, then used the costly box of alabaster to anoint Him. Thus she gave up the superstition that it was necessary to be buried with her tear bottle, plus she lowered herself to use her hair to wipe His feet. Since the woman's hair is her crowning glory, the symbolism here is significant: she humbled herself before the Savior. This is exactly what the Bishop told us.

It has been a blessing to me through the years since we first heard the "Eastern Customs," to find confirmation in many different places. I would certainly not desire to teach something about the Bible that is not true!

Here is one of the teachings which was the hardest for us to get straight at the time: In John 14, where Jesus was giving instructions to his disciples. "These are the words of the Eastern bridegroom," the Bishop told us.

Again, we were saying to ourselves, "*What?*" Most of us had sat through funerals where the pastor quoted this passage as a comfort to the mourners that the departed was now "in the arms of Jesus". But here the Bishop was saying that John 14 was part of the *marriage* ceremony.

He continued, "When he goes to prepare a place for them to live, he gathers as many of the wedding party and neighbors as he can find and speaks these words to the bride, beginning with 'let not your heart be troubled,' etc.

"If this had been a real bridegroom and bride, she would have given the following response, 'Yes, Lord, all that thou sayest I will do.' This is because during her instructions received from the priest, she was told that to have a happy marriage, she must treat her husband as if he were God."

Some of us, "women's libbers" at heart, did not care for this piece of advice. Someone said, "But we have all sinned and come short of the glory of God."

Someone else said, "In Christ we are neither Greek nor Jew, slave or free, male or female…"

And this third opinion: "If we treated our husbands like God, wouldn't he take advantage of us and we would be like doormats?"

The Bishop considered these statements for a moment. Then he said, "Suppose you knew Jesus was coming to supper tonight? How would your actions differ from what you do when you are only expecting your husband? Would you pick a fight with Jesus? How much quarreling would there be in your home if Jesus were the one coming to supper?"

One of the men said, "Paul said that women should keep silent in the church and learn from their husbands at home. What about that? And didn't Paul say he did not allow women to teach or have authority over men? And women are referred to as being the 'weaker vessel'."

The Bishop smiled his gentle smile, not in the least irritated with this burst of discussion. "That is true. But as for that last quote, my friend, Dr. George Lamsa, who translated the Bible from the Peshitta text, says it should read in that place, 'Hold the woman as a delicate vessel.'"

He added, "In the Book of Acts, there is also the question of Priscilla and Aquilla. According to protocol, his name should have been listed first in the text. Yet about half the time, her name came first. Nobody knows how that came to be, unless she was a member of royalty. But in that case, she would have been mentioned first *every* time. These are questions we do not know how to answer. Perhaps in the early church, they began to forget about protocol."

We also learned that according to Eastern thought, a wife is looked down upon if she cannot have children. They believe (as we do) that children are a blessing from God, but the Easterners think that if a woman has no children, then she has been cursed by Him.

A widow will seldom remarry in the East, unless she is passed along to someone else in the family, as we see in the account of Ruth and Boaz. It is a matter of property as much as anything else, because they do not want the wealth to be taken over by someone who is not a family member.

The bishop said, "Sometimes a childless widow will give her possessions to the temple and tell the family she is going on a pilgrimage. She will start walking, perhaps hundreds of miles toward some holy place. She will beg food along the way and sleep most anywhere. When she arrives at the holy place, she says a prayer and dies.

"These women are perfectly healthy, but there is nothing left for them to live for. They think that God has taken their husband as a curse to them, so they want to die. And if they can die in a holy place, they believe this will help them go to heaven."

The Bishop pointed out several examples of women in Bible times who were barren and suffered greatly until God blessed them with a child. Sarah, wife of Abraham, was so upset that she had not given him an heir that she arranged for Hagar to bear a child. Later, after it had "ceased to be with her after the manner of women," she gave birth to Isaac. Minoah's wife was barren, but by a promise of God she bore Samson. Elizabeth, the wife of Zacharias was barren, until she gave birth to a son of promise, John the Baptist.

Remember what Elizabeth said after she discovered that she was expecting John? "Thus hath the Lord dealt with me in the days wherein He looked on me, to take away my reproach among men." (Luke 1:25)

When the Bishop taught us these things, he commented that our culture was better in this respect, since widows are educated and usually are able to handle their own affairs. Barren women (by choice or by nature) are not ordinarily given a hard time by anyone except possibly the mother-in-law ("when are you going to make me a grandmother?).

Since there are several verses in the Bible where it may seem that even though the people themselves may have thought that they were cursed to have been childless or widowed, we should be assured that God does not curse anyone for these reasons. He is Spirit, and He loves and blesses the lives of all who belong to Him.

Chapter 7

SHEEP AND SHEPHERDS

"The Lord is my Shepherd" – this is one of the most beloved words of Scripture, cherished down through the ages. We think of the good shepherd, tenderly caring for his sheep, wisely meeting their needs for green pastures, still waters, and the like...

Imagine my surprise when, in recent years, Sunday School lessons and Christian magazines have presented a far different picture.

One recent Christmas there was this question: "Why were the shepherds at the manger?"

Bishop Pillai had told us that the reason, according to Eastern thought, was that shepherds were so highly thought of, that people would believe them when they "made known abroad the saying which was told them concerning this child" Luke 2:17.

However, recent articles and commentaries claim that the shepherds of Bible times were one of the "despised trades," had dubious moral sense (therefore not permitted in the temple); were smelly, scruffy outcasts, and altogether, not good people.

But, to answer the question as to why the shepherds were at the manger (Western commentators say "it's so that we would know that all are welcome at the manger.") Of course, all people are welcome at the manger!

If the shepherds were despised, immoral, outcast people, surely nobody in his right mind would have listened to them when they

23

told others what they had seen and heard concerning the angels' message and the babe in the manger.

When the Bishop taught us on this subject, he demonstrated the difference between the way the sheep and the goats graze in the fields. "The lambs wander anywhere, lose track of their mothers and the rest of the flock; nibble here and there until they might just fall over into a crevice.

"The goats, however, munch a few bites and then look up and all around; take a few more bites and look again."

We are all like sheep, we have gone astray, according to Isaiah 53:6. We need a shepherd to care for us."

The Bishop believed that it is important for us to know that the sheep were divided into three groups: the males of the first year, the females of the first year, and the rest of the flock. The owner's immediate family carefully shepherded the first two groups of sheep, giving them special care close to their home.

This special care is required especially in Jewish families because the male lamb of the first year that was offered at the Passover had to be without spot or blemish. If these lambs were not guarded carefully, they might become injured or bruised and thus not acceptable as an offering.

The Bishop said, "I believe that these three groups of sheep are the reason for the three questions and answers between Jesus and Peter which we find in John 21:15-17.

"Jesus says, 'Feed my lambs, feed my sheep, feed my sheep.' There were three kinds of flocks which Jesus was leaving to the care of Peter: the Jewish believers, the Gentile believers, and the pagans. Some commentaries try to say Jesus was testing Peter three times to see whether he would deny Him again: that is just guesswork and imagination. The Easterner who reads this verse immediately says, "Oh, yes; I understand: Peter is supposed to care for all three classes of the sheep in the flock.'"

When the shepherd takes the sheep out to the pasture in the morning, he takes along his food for the day, his staff and crook, and some smooth stones in his belt.

The stones are used in a sling by the shepherd to alert the sheep of impending danger. The sheep does not notice where he is going while grazing except to look a few inches away for better grass. When the shepherd notices that a sheep is wandering away, he calls to him by name.

If the sheep does not hear, the shepherd will sling a stone close by the mouth of the sheep without actually hitting the animal. The sheep will respond to the throwing of the stone and will then hear the shepherd calling him to come back to the flock.

The staff which the shepherd carries is a sort of club about 18 inches long, which hangs in his belt to be handy in case he must defend the sheep against animals or thieves.

The crook is a longer rod with a curve at the end, and with a sharp blade which he can use to reach up and get leaves from certain trees to feed the sheep with, in the event that there is no grass for them anywhere. All the other grazing animals may be starving, but the shepherd will not let the sheep go hungry.

"This crook of the shepherd is also a symbol of authority. I have seen bishops of the Eastern and Roman churches carrying this crook and blessing the people with it. I wonder if they understand that this is the symbol of the shepherd. The English word, 'pastor' means shepherd."

Sheep are so lacking in common sense that they will not drink from flowing water, since it usually makes a noise and frightens them. This is why Psalm 23 speaks of "still waters". If the shepherd cannot find a place where the waters are still, he must scoop out a pit in the sand for some water to run into and then the sheep can drink unafraid.

Sometimes the shepherd must lead his sheep across a little stream of water which they seem afraid to cross, so he must take one and toss him over, and the rest will jump across also. Sheep will follow one another blindly even when it is dangerous.

Sometimes, in spite of all the watchful care of the shepherd, a sheep will wander away and fall, perhaps getting his leg broken.

The shepherd always looks until he finds the sheep and carries him on his shoulders back to the sheepfold.

Another proof that shepherds were highly regarded by God is the number of shepherds in the Bible who were elevated to leadership. A shepherd must be a kind, thoughtful and wise person, or he will lose his flock. These are the qualities valued by God for leadership over His people.

Look at Ecclesiastes 12:11: "The words of the wise are as goads and as nails fastened by the master of assemblies, which are given from one shepherd." The Bishop said this refers to the wise men who would sit in the gate of the city and make judgments. When the shepherds came to town, he said, these elders of the city would invite them to sit with them and add to the discussion when decisions were to be made. The shepherd would stand his staff in the ground beside him so that his identity as a shepherd would be known.

The "master of assemblies" in the above verse would refer to the mayor or leader of the wise men in the gate. If there was some kind of dispute or debt which was pending, this master of assemblies would write it and fasten it with a nail to the walls of the gate. Whenever the matter was settled, the sheet would be folded up and again fastened with a nail.

This is what is meant in Isaiah 40:1,2 where it says, "Comfort ye, comfort ye, saith your God; speak ye comfortably to Jerusalem and cry unto her, that her warfare is accomplished, that her iniquity is pardoned: for she hath received of the Lord's hand double for all her sins."

In this case "double" does not mean that Israel has received twice as much punishment for her sins; indeed the context suggests that would not be the meaning. The "double" in this verse means that God has "doubled up" what the debt was written on, such as the ones in the gates of the city, folded them up and fastened them with a nail so that they cannot be seen any more by the passersby.

Jesus referred to Himself as the Good Shepherd, willing to lay down His life for his sheep. In John 10:7, He says, "Verily, verily I say unto you, I am the door of the sheep."

The sheepfolds in Eastern countries are made with rocks piled up in a circular shape and an opening which does not have a gate. When all the chores are done, the shepherd stretches himself across this opening and thus becomes the "door of the sheep" himself. If anyone tried to get into the sheepfold, he would have to go over the body of the shepherd.

When I was in Israel in 1988, I happened to look out the window of our tour bus, and saw this very thing: the sheep were in their sheep-fold, the shepherd was just putting out his fire, and as I watched, stretched himself across the opening. This opening was just wide enough for him to sit and rest his back against one side, and then he could touch the other side with his knees bent.

What a comfort it is to know that Jesus cares for us in the same way that a good shepherd cares for his sheep. It has been said that if sheep were subjected to the principle "survival of the fittest", they would be long gone from the planet.

Anyone who has ever owned sheep knows what silly creatures they are. One of my favorite pastors tells about the teacher who asked Johnny if he had ten sheep in a pen, and one got out, how many would he have left?

Johnny said, "None."

The teacher said, "You don't know much about math, do you?"

Johnny said, "And you don't know much about sheep."

A good shepherd gives his life for his sheep, and that is what Christ did for mankind. He is our door, the door to everlasting life.

"Do you see how beautiful is this picture of Christ as The Good Shepherd?" the Bishop concluded. "When we understand the way of life of the shepherd, it is more beautiful than we first realized, is it not?"

NOTE: Philip Keller wrote an inspiring book published by Zondervan in 1970: A Shepherd Looks at Psalm 23. Anyone who wishes to know more about the life of a Biblical shepherd should read this Christian classic.

Chapter 8

SEALED BY THE SPIRIT

"How many of you know what the Bible means when it says in Matthew 27:66: 'So they went, sealing the stone.'?" The Bishop began. (This is in reference to the stone which was placed in front of Jesus' tomb.)

We all hesitated to answer, because we had learned by now that what he was going to teach did not necessarily mean what we expected. As for myself, having been raised on a farm, I thought of the canning process for foods and how there was a rubber seal between the top of the jar and the lid which sealed out the air so the food would be preserved.

Thus, where the Bible says "sealing the stone" I imagined that the soldiers had stuffed something around the edges of the stone to keep the air out of the tomb. Fortunately, I managed to keep quiet this time.

"Do you know about signet rings?" he continued. "These have designs in them so that if you press the ring into clay or wax, it makes an impression.

"For instance, when Pharaoh gave Joseph a ring in Genesis 41:42, it was undoubtedly a signet ring, so that Joseph could take the authority over the land."

He then had us turn to Esther 3:10, where Haman received a ring from the king's hand with instructions to do with the Jews as he pleased. "Again, this should be a signet ring, as this is a symbol of authority, as we might say today, his power of attorney."

And in verse 12, it verifies that the orders to kill all the Jews in all the provinces were written in the King's name and sealed with his ring. [In 1973, the NIV was published which correctly adds "signet" to the word "ring" in both Genesis and Esther.]

Whenever a king issues an order with his seal, the Bishop pointed out, no man may reverse it, Esther 8:8, not even the king himself. Xerxes got around this dilemma by issuing another sealed order giving the Jews the right to fight to protect themselves, thus nullifying the effect of the first edict.

Isaiah speaks of a book being sealed, Isaiah 29:11, and in Jeremiah 32:10, we find that the prophet concluded a contract for property with witnesses who saw the money weighed in the balances, along with sealing the evidence.

Another reference to sealing with a signet is found in Daniel 6:17, "And a stone was brought, and laid upon the mouth of the [lions'] den; and the king sealed it with his own signet, and with the signet of his lords; that the purpose might not be changed concerning Daniel."

Looking back to the verse in Matthew, where it says that the soldiers sealed the stone, we now see that it would have been the seal of the Roman government. This would be a warning placed on the stone to discourage anyone from entering, under the threat of punishment from Rome.

Now there are several verses in the New Testament which refer to the believer being sealed. One of these in John 6:27, where Jesus said, "Labor not for the meat which perisheth, but for that meat which endureth unto everlasting life, which the Son of man shall give unto you: for him hath God the Father sealed."

II Timothy 2:19 says, "Nevertheless the foundation of God standeth sure, having this seal, The Lord knoweth them that are his." Notice that Paul uses the seal as a figure of speech.

The Apostle Paul makes a similar statement in his letter to the Ephesians: (1:13) "In whom [Christ] ye also trusted, after that ye heard the word of truth, the gospel of your salvation: in whom also, after ye believed, ye were sealed with the Holy Spirit of promise."

II Corinthians 1:22: "[God] hath also sealed us, and given the earnest [NIV: deposit] of the Spirit in our hearts."

The Bishop concluded: "If an earthly king is able to make a decree which no man can break, how much more will the King of Kings keep His promise? And for how long? Ephesians 4:30: "And grieve not the Holy Spirit of God, whereby ye are sealed unto the day of redemption."

I had been taking notes, but at the same time I noticed that our hostess, in whose home we were meeting, was fidgeting as if she wished to speak. The Bishop called on her. "Is there a problem?" he asked.

"Excuse me," she said hastily, rushing off to her bedroom. She emerged with a package of writing paper. "Look! This came from my sister yesterday."

The box contained sheets of paper, envelopes, a candle, and a design on the end of a handle. The instructions said that when one is ready to seal the envelope, you should melt a small portion of the candle across the flap, and press the design into the wax.

"What is the design?" someone asked.

"It's my initial. I've never had anything like it before. Isn't it amazing that it got here just in time to illustrate the lesson!"

I looked at the Bishop. "He confirmed the word with signs following?" I asked, quoting the last verse of the Book of Mark. He gave a little nod. "It would seem so," he agreed.

Chapter 9

SACKCLOTH, ASHES AND DUST

In India, as well as in other parts of the world, sackcloth, ashes and dust bring to mind mourning, repentance, and also sacrifice, the Bishop told us. These are symbols which are thousands of years old, known long before Christianity.

For instance, in Genesis 18:27, we find Abraham speaking of himself as "dust and ashes" in order to plead with God for Lot's family in Sodom. He humbled himself before God by calling himself only dust and ashes. This is typical of Eastern thought, the Bishop said, and is widely understood in that society.

"The act of sitting down in dust or ashes has this significance: When a man sits in the dust, he is saying, 'Lord, I came from the dust; to the dust I return. All shall return to the dust in death; but now, Lord, I return to the dust alive, in order to show my humility and repentance.'"

Ashes are symbolic of salvation to the non-Christian Gentiles: it means salvation by sacrifice. You may remember in Numbers 19, how the Israelites killed and burned a red heifer and made ashes of it. These ashes were used for a sin offering.

The Gentiles understood this symbolism also, for they would put dust and ashes all over their bodies and forehead, meaning: "Lord, please save me on the merit of this sacrifice of which these ashes are symbolic."

He explained, "If any Hindu puts ashes on his forehead in the morning before breakfast, that means he is saying to God, 'Lord, not on my merit, but on the merits of the sacrifice which is represented in the ashes, please forgive my sin. I will be protected, Lord, through this day on the merits of the ashes which I have on my forehead, which are the symbol of salvation by sacrifice.'"

He said the Hindus of his country believe in these ashes in the same way that Christians believe in the blood of Christ. Christians say they are covered with the blood; the Hindus say they are covered with ashes.

This is why, if a man in India has ashes all over his forehead, he is not really dirty; he is clean as anyone in another country. He has bathed, but he has put these ashes on his forehead. Westerners tend to think the man is dirty, but his own countrymen understand.

The Hindu also puts a little bit of ashes or dust on his lips and on his tongue. The Bishop said this means the man is saying to himself, "Not only do I put ashes on my body as a sort of protection, but I also put my insides under the protection of God by putting a little bit of ashes in my mouth."

In Psalm 102:9, David said, "I have eaten ashes like bread, and mingled my drink with weeping." This shows that he not only was taking the symbol of salvation into his body, but he was also weeping so continuously that the tears dropped into the water he was drinking.

In the Book of Job we find an example of a man who sat in the dust when he had lost everything in his life: all his sons and daughters, all his sheep and property. Everything was gone except his wife, who was such a grumbler that she was of no help to him anyway!

So Job, covered with sores and very miserable indeed, sat down in the dust to proclaim his mourning and his humility before God.

Sackcloth is spoken of as a symbol of mourning in a number of places in the Bible. One familiar reference is in Genesis 37:34 when Jacob was persuaded by his sons that their brother Joseph had been killed by a wild beast. Jacob then "rent his clothes, and put sackcloth upon his loins, and mourned for his son many days."

Sackcloth is also mentioned, along with dust, in the story of Jonah. This prophet was preaching to the wicked city of Nineveh, and then it says, "For word came unto the king of Nineveh and he arose from his throne and laid his robe from him, and covered him with sackcloth and sat in ashes." (Jonah 3:8)

The Bishop explained that sackcloth is a coarse material made of camel's hair or goat's hair and is worn as a sign of mourning. "Instead of a smooth cloth made of good material, we wear a coarse material made of camel's hair. We wear it when we fast, in order to manifest to God, that instead of good silk clothing, we wear the coarse clothing that will hurt the body. Clothes made of this coarse hair feels like pins pricking the skin. This way we think that God will know that our prayer is sincere."

He added, "When you go inside a Catholic church, you will see that they have holy water and the ashes also. They put a little bit in their mouths, for the same reason as the Hindus, as those who are Roman Catholic know." I never thought to ask him if his own Orthodox church also followed this custom.

He pointed out that the Hindu who has sinned must sit in dust and ashes, and pray and fast and mourn with sackcloth. But of course they will never find peace with God unless they forsake the man-made systems and look to the true God.

He said, "This is my stand, which I make concerning all the nations of the world. It is not by might, nor by power; it is not by sackcloth or ashes, nor by fasting and praying; but only by faith in Christ alone, by which man can be saved and find the peace of God."

Chapter 10

RAHAB THE "HARLOT"

Rahab is another example of wrong-headed thinking in the Western world, according to Bishop Pillai.

You may ask how he could possibly save the reputation of a woman who is plainly called a harlot in the Bible? She is found in the book of Joshua, where she hid the Israelite spies and sent them on their way safely. Why did she do this? Because she had heard that "the Lord your God, he is God in heaven above, and in earth beneath."

We also find Rahab listed in Chapter 11 of Hebrews, where a whole list of heroes of the faith are given. Most commentaries say that because Rahab helped the spies, she was accepted as a hero of the faith, even though she was a harlot.

But Bishop Pillai said that the word "harlot" in Eastern thought pertains to any woman who goes without a veil. The veil is God's protection over the woman, so that even today, a man would hesitate to strike a woman wearing a veil. They think that God would punish them if they did so.

The word translated "harlot", the Bishop explained, is a term which applies to any woman who deals with the public without her veil. This could be someone like a shop-keeper, a post-mistress, or an innkeeper.

In the case of Rahab, he believed that she was an innkeeper, since the Scripture says that her house was on the wall of the city, Joshua 2:15. In those days, the only person who had a house on the wall was the innkeeper, and this would be the first place the Israelites would go to spy out the city.

Most innkeepers were men in Bible times, he said, as in the case of Mary and Joseph at the birth of Jesus in Bethlehem. But sometimes the elders at the gate could not find a man to take the responsibility. Then perhaps a woman would come to the gate and say to the elders, "Let me be the innkeeper. I can do the job."

The elders would then say to her, "Well then, you must become 'harlot' since you cannot do the duties of the innkeeper and take care of the public with a veil over your face."

[The NIV translates "harlot" as "prostitute" three times in Joshua, and each case it has a footnote for that word: "or possibly an innkeeper".] The Bishop made a distinction between the two words: "harlot" meant anyone dealing with the public without a veil, while "prostitute" means just what we think it does today.

Some commentators know that Rahab was at the inn, but say that she must have been a prostitute there. After all, isn't that where the men go to find a prostitute today? [It's that Western thinking in evidence again!]

In Bible times men searched along the highway side, as illustrated by the story in Genesis 38 where Tamar "played the harlot" to trick Judah, her father-in-law, vs. 14. She was the widow of his oldest son, and the second son selfishly declined to marry her because any children she bore would inherit before him. So Judah then promised another son to her when he should be old enough.

Tamar discovered that this son had grown up but had not been given to her, so she went beside the road where she had learned that Judah would be traveling, wrapped in a veil, so he would think she was a prostitute. When Judah saw her beside the road, he did indeed think she was a prostitute and fell into her trap.

In addition, the provisions for privacy at the inn of that time in history were negligible. Travelers carried their own bedding with them, and often used their coats and cloaks to wrap themselves in.

When the innkeeper told Joseph there was "no room in the inn", he wasn't saying there were no vacant rooms. He meant there was no more space to spread out bedding on the floor!

When I was in Israel, our group saw the Good Samaritan Inn, part-way between Jerusalem and Jericho. It was one big open space...no separate rooms at all. Do you see how easily we think erroneous thoughts when we read the Bible? Somehow we must begin to think "Eastern", since most authorities, if they are honest, will agree that the Bible is an Eastern book. The problem is to apply this understanding to our study of the Scriptures.

Chapter 11

PUNISHMENT BY LAW

"Punishment and death are subjects about which we do not like to speak," the Bishop began his teaching one day, "and yet God uses examples about them in His Word to give us understanding about many spiritual truths."

"One example," he continued, "is found in Roman 7:24, where we find the words, "'O wretched man that I am! Who shall deliver me from the body of this death?'"

In the portion of Scripture just previous to this, Paul is explaining the difference between being under grace and being under the law. Paul wants to be delivered from the dead body which is like being under law, now that the reign of grace has been given by God.

In the East, the Bishop explained, a dead body has special significance, because this is involved in one form of punishment practiced in that part of the world.

Common types of punishment are, one: take a man upon a hill and throw him off; two: put a rope around his neck and hang him; three: put a man in prison, tie him to a dead body and leave him there for a week.

As horrible as this sounds, God uses this illustration to show us that if we are born again and refuse to renew our minds, continuing to walk after the flesh, then we are just like the prisoner who is tied to a dead body. That is what Paul is referring to when he says, "...who will deliver me from the body of this death?"

Paul is good at asking such a question and then answering it later with a theological statement. "For the law of the Spirit of life in Christ Jesus hath made me free from the law of sin and death."

The Apostle says it another way in his letter to the Galatians: "Stand fast therefore in the liberty wherewith Christ hath made us free, and be not entangled again with the yoke of bondage." This means that we need not be tied up with those things of the flesh, which are headed for death anyway.

Another verse pointed out to us by the Bishop pertaining to death, is found in Matthew 23:27, "Woe unto you, scribes and Pharisees, hypocrites! For ye are like unto whited sepulchers, which indeed appear beautiful outward, but are within full of dead men's bones, and of all uncleanness."

These sepulchers, the Bishop said, are graves which are kept white-washed. The bereaved relatives go out to the graveyard and wash off the tombstones, whitewash them and put on flowers. They are clean and lovely on the outside, but on the inside is decay and corruption.

Many people are like the Pharisees of whom Jesus speaks: they may look pious on the outside, but are defeated and full of agony and despair. We Christians should be filled instead with the fruit of the Spirit: joy, love, peace, gentleness, and so forth, so that we may be even more lovely on the inside than we are on the outside!

Many people received punishment or death in the Bible by stoning. This practice was set forth in the law as being required for those who were guilty of serious infractions of the law, especially those who were adulterers and those who worshiped other gods.

We find in the Scriptures, that stoning is described as being performed by the leaders and members of the synagogue. The method of stoning to death is not considered as one person killing another. The person throwing the stones believes that it is not he himself doing the killing of the accused one, but that it is the stone doing the killing. He knows that the law was written on stones, and the accused broke the law, so now the law by way of the stones is doing the killing.

When we read in Acts 7:58 about Stephen being stoned to death, we note that the stoning was done by several people and there were witnesses who laid down their clothes. We can see that this was an execution of the type provided by law.

Paul also was stoned, and we find in Acts 14:19 that certain Jews had persuaded the people that Paul was worthy of execution. After being stoned, he was left for dead outside the city, but as the disciples stood around him, he rose up and continued his journey. We can only assume that when the disciples gathered around Paul's body, that they must have prayed that he would live, and that the "prayer of faith would raise him up" according to James 5:15. The lesson for us is that no matter how defeated we may feel, or how much we feel tied to the things of this world, still God is able to deliver us out of these situations.

Easterners believe that when a person has transgressed against the law, it is impossible to hide from God. They think that God will track down that person to the ends of the earth, if necessary, so that justice will be done. This is why, in Eastern thought, it is logical that Judas killed himself. "He knew that God would get him sooner or later for his betrayal of the Lord," Easterners say, "So he just made it earlier by killing himself."

There are some curious examples of punishment in the Bible that are hard to understand unless we look at their symbolism. The people in the East think that anyone who has done wrong should have his punishment fit the crime.

An example of this is found in the latter portion of II Kings 9, which describes the horrible death of Jezebel, wife of King Ahab, an idolatress who threatened to kill the prophet Isaiah. First she was thrown down into the street and trampled on by a horse; when they went to bury her, they found that she had been eaten by dogs. An appropriate death, they thought, because dogs are among the most despised animals in Eastern society.

Another example of an appropriate death is found in Judges 4 in the story of Jael and Sisera. Jael and her husband Heber were Kenites, or neutrals in the war being fought nearby; Sisera, the commander of the Canaanite army fighting Israel, was fleeing from the battle. Jael invited him into the tent, and gave three marks of hospitality: she covered him with a mantle, which is symbolic of protection; she gave him food when he had only asked for water. When he asked her to stand in the door of the tent and if anyone came, she should say he wasn't there, she did not refuse.

In verse 21 the narrative rather abruptly states that Jael has taken a tent stake and hammer and has driven it through his temple. The key to understanding this situation is found in verse 22. It says that Sisera was found in HER tent. Whenever anyone is living in tents, the Bishop explained, there must be a private place for the women. There is the main part of the tent, and there is at least a hanging for privacy within the main tent, or perhaps a separate tent for the women.

When we see that Sisera has placed himself in this private part of the tent, he endangered Jael's life. If her husband should come home and find a strange man in her private quarters, he could easily think the worst of her.

At this point in the story, Jael may well have said to herself, "I gave him three indications of hospitality, but he didn't believe me. To make himself doubly safe, he has invaded my private space, and this may save his life but not mine." Thus, we see that the stake through Sisera's temple is symbolic of his dying because of his wrong thinking. He did not believe Jael's gestures of hospitality, so it is only appropriate, in Eastern thought, that he should die with a stake through his temple!

Chapter 12

OUR DAILY BREAD

Eastern bread, the Bishop told us during the 1960s, is not like the long loaves which we buy in the bake shop or grocery store, sliced to make toast or sandwiches. The bread then, and also in many parts of the world today, is a flat round bread which looks like a pancake.

He explained to us that when we read the parable about the guest who arrived at night and the host borrowed three loaves of bread, (Luke 11:5-7) our mental machinery would tend to click over to our own kind of bread.

Since he told us about the Biblical bread, though, the American diet has expanded to include such delicacies as pita bread and tortillas. Thus, when I teach about Eastern bread these days, students have no problem with the concept.

The bread in his native India, he said, is called "chapatties", made with wheat flour and water, and baked over hot coals or on hot rocks. Three of these "loaves" of bread would be just about right to feed a hungry traveler arriving in the middle of the night.

In verse 11 of the same chapter of Luke, we see another reference to bread. "If a son shall ask bread of any of you that is a father, will he give him a stone?"

The beauty and aptness of this phrase in not appreciated by those of us who do not know the customs of the typical Eastern household. These round discs of bread are stacked up after being made, and then a round stone just the same size as the bread is placed on top of them to hold the stack in place.

When they first begin to use this stone it may be white, but gradually it becomes discolored by the bread, and handling of it, so that eventually the stone begins to look almost exactly like the bread.

Do you see how this explains the verse which says, '...will he give him a stone?' It is not just any stone which is meant, but the stone which holds down the bread, and could be mistaken by a careless person.

"But this verse says that our heavenly Father is even more careful than earthly fathers who know how to give good gifts to their children, and will give the Holy Spirit to them who ask Him, and will not make any careless mistake about it."

It is also significant that Jesus used bread to set in place the covenant of communion. He referred to himself as the bread of life, John 6:35, and the "living bread which came down from heaven; if any man eats of this bread, he shall live forever... John 5:51."

It is interesting to see how many times in the Bible we find bread used as a figure of speech:

Bread of affliction, Deuteronomy 16:3

Bread of tears, Psalm 80:1

Bread of wickedness, Proverbs 4:17

Bread of deceit, Proverbs 20:17

Bread of idleness, Proverbs 31:27

Bread of adversity, Isaiah 20:30

Besides this, there are a number of verses in the Bible regarding leavened and unleavened bread. The leavened bread is always associated with undesirable things. For example in Matthew 16:6 Jesus says "Beware of the leaven of the Pharisees." Later, in I Corinthians 5:7, Paul says, "Cleanse out the old leaven that you may be a new lump, as ye are unleavened."

The Bishop stressed that these are good comparisons because of the nature of the wheat flour which is used to make the bread.

Flour which is freshly ground has rising properties within itself, and no leavening is needed to make light bread with it.

"Each housewife was supposed to grind her grain fresh every day," he explained. But if she wanted to be free from the task of grinding for a few days, she would grind enough in one day to last for several days.

"However, on the second day, the flour would not rise as well as when it was fresh, so the housewife would have to use leavening to make the bread rise. Bread with leavening it was therefore regarded as having foreign or unclean properties: the mark of the lazy housewife.

"I sometimes think this is the way we go about reading the word of God. We read a little bit one day and think it will last us for several. But, on the second day, yesterday's reading is stale." He concluded, "Let us resolve to read God's precious word every day. It will be refreshing to us, and a blessing to our soul continuously."

After the Bishop's death, I began to teach his material. Once, in a private home in St. Clairsville, Ohio, I was holding forth on the subject of bread. My friend Erma Lodge, who was my prayer partner at that time [I believe a pastor's wife should have a prayer partner *outside* the congregation] was smiling all through the lesson. I began to wonder why she was smiling so much. I didn't stop teaching and call on her, because I knew she would break in if it were important.

I made my final remarks and turned to Erma to see what had tickled her so much. She turned over a little stack of devotional booklets she had brought to share with the group. The cover featured a beautiful color picture of a loaf of bread and a cup of wine.

Again, the Lord had confirmed His word with signs following!

Chapter 13

MORE CULTURE CLASHES

Once when I had completed what I thought was enough writing for Bishop Pillai to check over, I called the home where he was staying and asked if he would be there that afternoon.

His hostess checked with him, and the arrangement was made. My three older children were in school, so I had my youngest with me. The Bishop answered the door, and invited us in. I looked around and could not see anyone else in the house. Aware by now of the customs of concerning women in his society, I said, "Oh, Mrs. Brown isn't here?"

"No, she has gone for groceries," he said, and then an expression of extreme discomfort came over his face. He had arranged for a woman to whom he was not related to be alone with him, something which he would never have done in his own society.

By now I was getting a little tired of the restrictions which his way of life presented, and I made up my mind that I would not be hindered with the task of producing his manuscript, customs or no customs. Taking a chair in the living room, I pulled my little one onto my lap, and handed over the work which I had accomplished so far.

At the outset, it had been the Bishop's wish that I take down his teachings during his appearances. In order to garner enough material, his friends and supporters had also arranged for small group meetings in homes to fill in between public meetings in churches. I soon realized that it would have been improper for the two of us to meet privately anywhere for him to tell me what he wanted in the book.

Now, as he looked over the pages which I had brought him, he engaged in an occasional "Hmmmph" as something struck him. I wanted to say, "What, what?" but managed to be quiet until he was finished. At one point, he laughed out loud. "No, no, that is not the word I meant," he said, marking it with his pen. "English is not my first language, you know. No wonder you could not understand me...the word was very close, though."

When he had finished, I was ready with a question which I had just been aching to ask him. I had asked other people this question, and they said the Bishop would not discuss it. But I had made up my mind that if I was willing to write his book for him (and not charge him anything for it, at that) he should be willing to give me an answer.

I was expecting him to tell me two names which would be long and unpronounceable, which he had shortened to initials for the sake of convenience.

"Bishop, what do the initials "K" and "C" stand for in your name? I notice you never use your full name." He gazed at me thoughtfully for a moment, then answered, "When my parents named me, they gave me names of Hindu gods. When I became a Christian, I did not wish to use those names any more, because it would be like calling on the names of those gods. So I merely use the initials."

It had been a struggle to understand him and his society, and this day I felt that I had come a little closer to Eastern thought. But I was still to make many more mistakes in the weeks to come. Fortunately, the Bishop was kind and patient when my efforts went awry. But that day was the only time I was ever alone with him, and even then I had a child on my lap. With all these rules which we had to follow, it is a wonder that we ever got the job done!

I had visualized a young Pillai going to England to be educated, and learning something about the "civilized" world.

Imagine our surprise when he told us that in his view, our western culture was the one which should be called "pagan". As he began to learn Christian precepts, as a new believer, he became even more resentful of the British. Previously his people had chafed under the 'superior' British rule, but now he was learning how Christians should behave.

"The British missionaries came to India supposedly to convert our people to Christ. But we saw them playing tennis with the officers in their clubs, driving nice automobiles, putting their children in English schools, and hiring four or five natives to cook, clean, and mind their children –- at starvation wages, at that. They merely served as chaplains to the English-speaking community.

"The people in England who gave sacrificially to support these men in the so-called mission field had no idea that very few if any Indians were ever converted as a result of their work. We knew that they referred to us as pagans, but we thought of ourselves has having a rich cultural heritage. We saw that they did not follow Jesus' teachings to be meek and lowly, but rather lorded it over us." It was obvious that the young Pillai had to learn to forgive the British whom he felt had wronged his people. He had worked through his resentment, and through many years had graciously taught Biblical truths to all those willing to listen. But, every once in awhile, we could see a glimpse of his former attitude peeking through.

Chapter 14

MEET ME AT THE GATE

The Bishop taught us that in the Eastern world, the gates of the city have tremendous importance. Around each city there was a wall, tall and wide, and usually just one gate, except for Jerusalem which has 12 gates. Because the wall was wide, the depth of the gate was sufficient for a number of people to sit there. Traditionally, the "elders of the gate" gathered here to make decisions, settle disputes and generally give advice.

Remember that in those days, the elderly people were much honored and revered, so that their opinions were solicited in matters of importance. We see this in the Book of Ruth, where Boaz wished to arrange to take Ruth (and her property), and went to the elders in the gate to settle the matter, Ruth Chapter 4.

We see this wording many times in the Bible, and sometimes fail to realize their importance, because in our day and time we do not have walled cities and their gates.

There is also usage of gates as a figure of speech. Job and Psalms both speak of the "gates of death"; we also see "the gates of thy land shall be set wide open", and "gates of the rivers" are spoken of. Anyone who is described as sitting in the gate may be presumed to be a worthy person. In Genesis 19 we read that Lot sat in the gate of Sodom, and when he saw the two angels coming toward him, he bowed and invited them into his home. From that time to this, men of the East would go sit in the gate of the city and hope to entertain "angels unaware".

Notice the first answer the angels gave to Lot: "Nay, but we will abide in the street all night," This is the appropriate answer according to the folkways in the East. The courteous answer must be a refusal, just in case the prospective host has offered his hospitality at an awkward time. But when Lot "pressed on them greatly" they finally agreed to be his guests. Then we see Matthew 16:18 where Jesus said to Peter, "...upon this rock I will build my church and the gates of Hell shall not prevail against it."

This presumes, you see, that Hell is a walled city with a gate where all the most wicked devils sit, hatching plans to destroy the righteous.

Chapter 15

LET'S BE SALTED

The Rev. Paul Crockett of the Old Town Methodist Church, where we had first heard Bishop Pillai speak, called to say that he was returning to administer the "covenant of salt".

"The WHAT covenant?" I asked.

"Oh, you haven't heard the teaching on the covenant of salt? You're really going to enjoy this."

I wasn't so sure. I knew about the blood covenant, of course, but what about salt? However, I gathered my note-taking materials, my husband (bless him!) agreed to baby-sit, and I was off to Old Town.

Several people were there who had heard this teaching before, and had requested that the Bishop give us an opportunity to make this covenant. Since I was not the consummate Bible scholar, I had not even heard there was such a thing.

"Sounds pagan," someone had muttered under his breath, and I in truth wondered where this teaching was going. Roman soldiers were paid in bags of salt, which they could use to barter, since salt was so valuable then. This is where we get our word "salary". And sometimes we use it as a figure of speech, as in "Did he earn his salt doing that job?" or "Is she worth her salt?"

I should have been more trusting, because right there in Numbers 18:19, and in II Chronicles 13:5, the Lord promises to make a covenant of salt forever with the Israelites, and with the house of David, respectively.

"Anyone who eats salt together has made this covenant," the Bishop began. "This is why it was so disgraceful when Judas had enjoyed the hospitality of Jesus all that time, and then went out and betrayed him. Such a person only deserves death, and this may well be why Judas took his own life. They believed that a person would have his life taken by God anyway because of this sin, so they may as well take their own life and get it over with."

The new understandings which we got from his teachings were found in Matthew 5:13, "Ye are the salt of the earth, but if the salt have lost his flavor, he is good for nothing but to be cast out and trampled under the feet of men."

The Bishop said, "Salt means truthfulness." Many of us had heard sermons on how salt is a figure of speech in the Bible for PRESERVATION. Now we had to get this new thought in our minds.

"The salt which they use in the kitchens is like rock salt, which is stored in jars. The kitchens have stone floors, which are washed by swishing water over them, so that in time, the salt in the bottom of the jar gets leached out and has no more taste of salt in it.

"They don't just throw it away anyplace, you see; they put it out on the highway to be trampled underfoot to symbolize that if you have lost your truthfulness, you are no longer of any use.

"Then in the Gospel of Mark, chapter 9, verse 50, Jesus is quoted as saying that we should have salt in ourselves. We should be truthful, it means."

When several other illustrations had been given, the Bishop moved to the communion table, where a lovely dish containing salt had been placed.

"Please come forward and take a little pinch of salt to put on your tongue. As you taste the salt, make your promises to God that you will be truthful and honest toward Him and your fellow-man; and that you will have salt in yourselves, as the Bible says we should do."

It was a solemn occasion, and several people lingered at the communion table to consider what had been taught to us that evening and how they should apply it to their lives.

Someone said, "Man, when I put that salt on my tongue, it stung my mouth."

His friend said, "Maybe God is giving you an extra taste of the salt so you will remember what you promised here!"

Chapter 16

JUST AND UNJUST STEWARDS

The Bishop told us that the duties of the Eastern steward is another area which is misunderstood by Western Christians. In Luke 16:1, we have Jesus beginning a parable this way, "And he said also unto his disciples, 'There was a certain rich man, which had a steward; and the same was accused unto him that he had wasted his goods.'"

The Bishop explained that in Eastern society, this steward is much more than the American farm manager would be. He is usually a relative, and is brought into the household under a Covenant of Salt (See chapter, "Let's Be Salted").

The steward becomes a member of the family and has authority over all members of the home except, of course, the master. He has the master's signet ring and thus has authority to sign documents, hire and fire servants; even correct the master's wife if she is wrong, and to spank the children. He pays rent and taxes, forgives debts and lends money; he can buy and sell property. All these actions are legal since he has the trust of the master of the household.

Because he is under the covenant of salt, this steward has taken a sacred oath and can be trusted to do no wrong willingly. The master does not pay the steward by check periodically, as we would in the Western world; rather, they both know that the steward will take a certain percentage of the business transactions...whatever amount the steward feels is rightfully due to him for his labor.

Luke 16:2: "And he called him, and said unto him, 'How is it that I hear this of thee? Give an account of thy stewardship; for thou mayest be no longer steward.'"

The Bishop explained that the master is asking for an accounting of the books, indicating that if he is not satisfied, the steward might lose his position.

Verse 3: "Then the steward said within himself, 'What shall I do? For my lord taketh away from me the stewardship; I cannot dig; to beg I am ashamed.'"

This steward is alarmed because he is not a common laborer. He is well-educated and too proud to beg for a living.

Verse 4: "I am resolved what to do, that, when I am put out of the stewardship, they may receive me into their houses."

We see here that the steward has decided he will do what he knows is honest and above reproach. Then if the master fires him anyway, he still will have been honest in his dealings, and perhaps one of his master's customers will give him another stewardship.

Verse 5, "So he called every one of his lord's debtors unto him, and said unto the first, 'How much owest thou unto my lord?'"

This means, the Bishop explained that the steward is putting the books in order by going over the debts.

Verse 6, "And he said, 'A hundred measures of oil.' And he said unto him, 'Take thy bill and sit down quickly, and write fifty.'"

The debtor owed 100 measures, and the steward kept fifty for his share.

Verse 7, "Then said he to another, 'And how much owest thou?' And he said, 'A hundred measures of wheat.' And he said unto him, 'Take thy bill and write fourscore.'"

This debtor owed 100 measures of wheat, and out of this the steward reserved 20 for himself, and left 80 (fourscore) to his master. Today we might say he kept a 20 percent commission on the wheat, a just share for his work as steward, which he had a right to negotiate under the covenant of salt.

If the steward had been dishonest, the Bishop explained, he could have stolen a large amount of the master's wealth and run away. It would be a temptation, since he was accused of wrongdoing already. But according to the custom, he was collecting his fair share of what had been produced under his stewardship.

Verse 8 continues, "And the lord commended the unjust steward, because he had done wisely: for the children of this world are in their generation wiser than the children of light." The fact that the lord praised him proves that these dealings were honest. The Bishop said that if the steward had broken the covenant of salt, he would have been disgraced and subject to death as a traitor, and the parable would have ended that way if that had been the point that Jesus was making.

But the truth which Jesus wished to stress is found in the next verse (Luke 16:9), "And I say unto you, Make to ourselves friends of the mammon of unrighteousness, that, when ye fail, they may receive you into everlasting habitations..." The first part of this verse, "...Make to yourselves friends of the mammon of unrighteousness" means that we as Christians should make use of the prerogatives of this world: the privileges, power, the knowledge, education, wealth and so forth, to bring about good things, and the things of God. "...when ye fail, they may receive you into everlasting habitations" means that when you die (fail) and are born again to everlasting life, you will have your reward. If you are faithful in the unrighteous mammon (worldly goods) then you are entitled to the true wealth of spiritual riches.

Then in Verse 13 of the same chapter, it says, "Ye cannot serve both God and mammon." God is the one power which is good; Satan is one power which is evil. We may know that we should despise the evils that lurk in our minds, such as tempers, grudges, love of gossip; sometimes we grow quite attached to them.

But we cannot serve both God and these evils at the same time and enjoy peace with God. Christ came that good would have dominion over evil and give us peace. A mind in harmony with Christ serves only God.

The Bishop reminded us that we can choose to be just or unjust stewards as followers of the Lord. It is possible to pretend to have much religion, like the scribes wanting to spoil the widows' houses, but not be trustworthy at all.

Having a Sunday religion does not make us a trustworthy person. We must have Christ within us, and the renewed mind of Christ. Then we have light, truth, and loyalty toward God. Having Christ within us should become a way of life. If we are faithful stewards by our prayers for others, by our giving of material blessings as well as the ministry of the Word, we will have laid up treasures in heaven where they may not rust or corrupt. Thus, when we are called before God for an accounting, we will be commended for being wise and just stewards. We can look forward to those wonderful words, "Well done, thou good and faithful servant." (Matthew 21:25)

Chapter 17

HOW THEY GOT MARRIED

One of the most difficult concepts which the Bishop taught us was that marriages were arranged in Bible times, and still are even today in Middle Eastern countries.

He introduced the subject with the story of how Abraham sent his trusted servant back to his homeland to find a bride for Isaac. "Nobody would arrange a marriage for me!" I thought to myself. I had already concluded that women were treated like property in those days, which I didn't like, and this was just one more example of it.

"How do the women feel about having their marriages arranged?" I asked.

"They are taught from the earliest age that this is God's will for their lives. They believe that their marriage was made in heaven before the foundation of the world, and that someday a matchmaker will discover God's will and the marriage will be arranged for them. They are taught that this is not only the spiritually proper thing to do, but also that it is very romantic."

Just as I was turning over in my mind how "romantic" it would be to marry someone you never saw before, he added, "In the case of Rebekah, you remember, she could have refused to go. Her family let her decide if she wished to become Isaac's wife." (Gen. 24:57.)

Not only did I have trouble getting this concept well in mind, but I have had trouble teaching it ever since. One problem has been that the translators of modern versions of the Bible have insisted on translating Matthew 1:18 "when Mary was espoused to Joseph" as "when she was engaged..." The Bishop kept reminding us that there was no such thing as an engagement in Bible times.

Some of our confusion comes when we fail to associate "espoused" with "married": according to their customs, they had signed the marriage agreement but had not yet "come together". In our society, if people get married and fail to come together, it is grounds for an annulment.

However, in Eastern countries it is common for people to sign the marriage contract and not come together until they are old enough, or until an astrologer has cast their horoscopes and settled on a favorable time.

In Matthew 1:20, I often point out to modern-day students, it says that the angel said to Joseph, "fear not to take unto thee Mary thy wife..." You see how the angel refers to Mary "his wife". One time I did an experiment: I asked various people to read that passage aloud just to see how many of them would say, "fear not to take unto thee Mary AS thy wife." Almost all of them added the "as" because we have the mindset that they were not yet married. Unfortunately, most modern translations put in the "as" even though it is not in the Greek text.

I once wrote to the publishers of one of the "today-versions" and said: "Surely you know that you are in error to say that Mary and Joseph were engaged, and before they could get married, she was found to be pregnant. Our young people read this and get the wrong idea. They come to me and ask why we make a big deal about unwed mothers, since Mary was one. Couldn't you put in a well-placed footnote explaining that the marriages were arranged?"

"Yes," they wrote back, "we understand all that, but we didn't think it was significant. We wanted to place the story in today's setting to make it more real to the readers."

In one class which I was teaching, different versions of the Bible were being used, and one young woman had the one which used the phrases containing "engaged", "pregnant", etc. She looked at the text in dismay. "You mean I can't trust what my Bible says?" she exclaimed. Such are the difficulties in teaching something different from the standard fare being put forth from the modern publishers. In my experience, the King James translators seem to be the only ones who did not have some kind of ax to grind.

Not long after I completed the Bishop's material, a friend called to say that an Indian student needed the proper blouses to wear with her sari. She was not able to purchase the right kind; would I sew some for her?

"Certainly," I replied, thinking I could sneak in a question about whether her family had arranged a marriage for her that she would be forced to enter upon returning home. Could she do this, I wondered, after seeing the freedom which we enjoy here in America?

After waiting politely until the blouse problem was explained, I got around to the marriage business. Had her family arranged a marriage for her, which she would honor when she returned?

"Oh, yes," she answered. "I haven't met him, but he comes from a very fine family. He is getting his education in England now."

"It doesn't bother you that all this has been arranged for you without your permission?" I couldn't help asking.

She looked at me in surprise. "No, I think it is wonderful to have it all settled. My family knows what is best for me. I don't have to compete for men's attentions as American girls do. The poor things are so nervous and upset as to whether they will find a husband. They spend much time on their appearance and clothing, while I can concentrate on my studies and know everything has been arranged." I looked at her, and sure enough, she did not wear any make-up and her hair was worn in one long braid down her back.

After hearing from the Bishop that these marriages were sometimes made when the principals were mere children, I began to wonder how long ago the arrangement had been in place for this woman, who was now a college student.

"So, how long ago was the marriage arranged, and how old are you now?" I blurted out.

I shouldn't have asked that question. She looked very embarrassed. Evidently one's age was not to be discussed, so I hastily returned to the subject of the blouses. Another gaffe!

The Bishop had emphasized the spiritual significance of arranged marriages: Christ had referred to himself as the Bridegroom, and we as the Church are the bride. God chose us before the foundation of the world to belong to Him.

The foretold marriage supper of the Lamb is one of the most cherished promises that we have from our Savior. All these figures of speech relating to marriages pertain to that time when we shall go in with Him to this feast.

Now when we read Matthew 22, we can understand that parable which has escaped us as Westerners, as we see how the man without a wedding garment was cast into outer darkness. If he had been wearing "the garment of salvation" and "the robe of righteousness" he could have come in to the feast.

Also, in Matthew 25, we have the well-known parable of the ten virgins, five of whom had failed to bring oil for their lamps. In the Bible, oil is a symbol of the Holy Spirit. When we receive Christ into our hearts, we have the Holy Spirit within us. Those five virgins who had no oil in their lamps had not received Christ, and therefore they were not recognized as belonging to the Bridegroom. How precious this is when we finally see it through the eyes of the Eastern people.

Chapter 18

THE DINNER THAT FAILED

During the time I was writing for the Bishop, I decided to invite him to dinner. I contacted the wife of a former missionary to India for recipes. I invited a guest I hoped he would enjoy meeting. I instructed the children to be on their best behavior. I even inquired as to his favorite dessert, and learned that he preferred to end a meal with fruit (so much for baking a fancy dessert).

We sat down to eat, and my husband asked the Bishop to say the blessing. I proudly began to pass the dishes: curried lamb, lentils, freshly baked bread...and all of us tried to keep a pleasant conversation going. But, not the Bishop. Without speaking, he bent over his plate. If he did respond to anyone, it was in monosyllables.

Being unaware that the Bishop was following another Eastern custom pertaining to eating habits, I was perplexed. Had I done something to offend him? I sent questioning looks to my husband, who answered with a shrug. Not knowing how to prepare the fruit he requested, I had placed several kinds in a bowl, so he could select something which he preferred.

The children soon asked to be excused. The Bishop took an apple from the bowl and said, "Let us go into the living room where we can talk." He must have seen the expression on my face, because as soon as he had settled himself in a chair, he began to explain, "In my country, you know, we do not talk while we are eating. In fact, only the dearest and closest friends eat together. If people invite someone to a meal that they do not know well, they feed them in a separate place from the rest of the family."

By this time I had been to many meetings to take notes for the manuscript, and had begun to get the gist of Eastern thinking, or so I thought. But this was something new. "Is there someplace in the Bible where this is illustrated?" I asked. "Oh, yes: you remember in Revelation 3:20 where Jesus said, 'Behold, I stand at the door and knock; if any man hear my voice, and open the door, I will come in to him and will sup with him, and he with me.'"

"So if people don't eat together unless they are well acquainted, the last part of verse 20 is a promise to the believer that we can expect to be intimate friends with Him?" He said, "Yes, and this is why it was so significant when my family met me at the ship, on my return to India. The reconciliation included a fine meal at which we all sat down and ate together. If we had still been estranged and had just met someplace, we would never have eaten at the same table."

Later I saw a picture in a magazine showing Mahatma Gandhi eating with some guests. He was sitting cross-legged at a low table, while the guests could be seen at a table through an archway. I thought of the latter portion of the book of Mark where it states that the believers went forth and preached everywhere, and the Lord working with them, confirming the word with signs following.

[That was the first time I noticed that the Lord sometimes confirms His word "with signs following". It wasn't that I didn't believe the Bishop's teaching, exactly; I just had a hard time visualizing the idea of having someone to a meal and not eating with them. The picture of Gandhi helped me to see how the meal was arranged. Since that time, having the Lord "confirm His word with signs following" has happened to me many times while teaching the Eastern Customs, and it is such a blessing. I praise God every time it happens.]

The Bishop said to us, "I had a big adjustment to make when I went to England to seminary, and their eating habits were just one of them," he said. "For instance, the British are such fools over their dogs. I was astonished when I saw the way dogs are treated there."

"You don't have dogs as pets in India?" I asked.

"I remember being permitted to play with puppies on the verandah, but when they got older we were not allowed to touch them. They were considered to be unclean and dangerous. If you think about it, the Bible doesn't have anything good to say about dogs, either: 'the dog returns to his vomit', and so forth.

"But we take good care of our animals. They are vaccinated, bathed, trained. Most dogs are not allowed to just run wild."

"Yes, I know all that, but when I go in someone's home and a dog jumps up on the couch beside me, I cannot help but cringe," he admitted.

I was relating this later to the lady whose family was hostess to the Bishop at that time, and she agreed that he did not seem to like their dog, even when her children tried to coax him to pet her.

"Let me just warn you about one thing," she said. "If he asks to borrow money, you can just kiss it goodbye. Evidently it says somewhere in the Bible that if someone asks to borrow, you should just give it to him. Several people have found out that when the Bishop says "borrow", he means "give".

Sure enough, in due time, we got a letter from the Bishop from the King George Hotel in New York City which was evidently his headquarters when he was in that area. Would we send him $100?

I told my husband what the lady had said about how the Bishop "borrowed". He said, "If you want to send him some of the money we have set aside for contributions, we should just say to ourselves that we will not expect it to be returned to us. That way, we won't keep wondering when he's going to pay it back."

I wrote a check for $100 and sent it. Three years later, after my husband had resigned his position as a physicist at Wright-Patterson Air Force Base and entered seminary, we received a letter from Bishop Pillai. It was a note saying he heard we had made this move, and he enclosed a check for $100!

Fast-forward to about 1988, when I was on the staff at Christian Retreat in Florida. Our ministry head, Dr. Gerald Derstine, had returned from one of his trips to Israel, and was telling us about taking a meal in an Arab home.

"They eat with their hands," he related. "They told me that they wash their hands thoroughly so they know they are clean. They don't trust spoons or other silverware, because who knows where they have been? But they know their hands are clean.

"They said that their Father Abraham ate this way, and if it was good enough for him, it was fine for them. They tear off a piece of their flat bread and make a little scoop out of it and dip it into a common dish of lamb and yogurt gravy."

"They all eat out of the same dish?" we asked in wonderment.

"Yes, and not only that, but the host said to me when we first sat down, 'Brother Gerald, I am going to do something first which is our custom, to show the others that you are my honored guest. I will take a piece of bread and dip it into the gravy and put it in your mouth, before the rest of us begin to eat. When a guest receives the "Bite of Honor", it shows that he is the special guest at the meal.'"

Someone said, "Oh, this is just like Jesus giving Judas the sop at the Last Supper – but was Judas an honored guest?"

"That's the supreme example of loving your enemies!"

It was fascinating to see the Biblical ways still being followed in the present time. It helped us to see what Jesus meant when He promised that He would come in and sup with us, and we with Him.

That is a dinner which cannot fail.

Chapter 19

EAGLES

Many students have told me that one of their favorite verses of Scripture has to do with renewing one's strength like the eagle. "Are you referring to Psalm 103:5, where it says 'thy youth is renewed like the eagle'?" I would ask them. Isaiah 40:31 also speaks of mounting up with wings as eagles.

To pique their interest about their favorite verse, I often asked them, "Will you still be as enthusiastic about the eagles when you read Micah 1:16, where it ways, 'Make thee bald, and poll thee for thy delicate children; enlarge thy baldness as the eagle...'?"

When I have their attention, I can launch into one of the Bishop's favorite teachings about eagles. Becoming bald as the eagle, as stated in Micah, is a puzzle until we find out about the eagle which is native to Mid-East countries. Bishop Pillai said that we don't have such a bird in the Western world.

This eagle is considered to be a holy bird by the people, because of the company he keeps: he makes his nest in the palm tree, which they believe is a holy tree. As Godly people, we should keep company with those who have a good influence on us.

But this bird also does something which the people believe to be very exemplary. Every so often he would begin to look old and dirty, and he would need to molt and grow some new feathers. However, for some reason the feathers do not easily detach themselves when he is ready to shed them, so in desperation he begins to fly up in higher and higher circles. Then he dives down into a patch of water, and the force of striking the water causes the old dirty feathers to come off.

The people believe that it is good luck to see the eagle divest himself of his feathers and so they gather to see it. They believe there is a parallel between the eagle getting rid of his feathers, and a person who wishes to "turn over a new leaf" and give up all his bad old ways to start over again.

The people see the eagle out there in the water, struggling to get to shore and to find some vegetation to hide under until his feathers can grow back. The godly people of the area bring food for the bird, because they are so impressed with his determination to get rid of all the old ways and make a fresh start.

The Bishop enjoyed this portion of his teachings, because you could see the twinkle in his eye as he would say, "Did the eagle look at some of his feathers and say, 'this one is not so dirty; I think I'll keep it'? No, the eagle says, 'I will make a clean sweep of the whole thing. I will start over; I will let the Godly people feed me until I can grow clean new feathers.'"

He told us that there are two kinds of eagles in the East: one is the "holy" eagle just mentioned; and the other is a "dirty" eagle, which we would call a vulture; these gather around any dead animal and eat it, as Jesus described in Matthew 24:28, "For wheresoever the carcass is, there will the eagles be gathered together."

The Bishop told us, "When a fasting Hindu breaks his fast, the first thing he wants to look at is a holy eagle. If he sees a dirty eagle instead, he goes back and fasts again. To the Hindu, it is an evil omen to break a fast without seeing a holy eagle."

He likened the vultures to carnal Christians who are always looking to material things. Their vision is not high enough because their believing is not high enough. They have pleasure in material things instead of looking to spiritual matters.

The Bishop explained that the holy eagles never eat anything that is dead; they seek out only live things for food. They build their nests in the tops of coconut palms, perhaps 80 or 90 feet off the ground. They are like the true believers who are saved by grace: the believers whose home is not of this world, but whose home is heavenward.

The Apostle Paul wrote to the Ephesians about being dead in our sins, but Christ has quickened us and raised us up to sit together in heavenly places in Christ Jesus, Ephesians 2:5,6.

According to this, we are already seated in heavenly places with Him. We were crucified with Him; we were buried with Him; we arose with Him, and we ascended with Him. These are very wonderful and thrilling thoughts for us to consider.

Easterners believe that the holy eagles are likened to heavenly beings. They are the "king of the birds", they say.

After the godly people feed the eagles, in six or seven weeks, the new feathers have grown out and they fly back to the treetops. Nothing can stop them now. That is why "they that wait upon the Lord shall renew their strength; they shall mount up with wings as eagles."

When we accept Christ as our Lord, we must examine ourselves, because we should be willing to say, "Lord, break me, melt me, mold me and take away any wicked feather of unbelief in my heart, and remove any old feathers that have made me weak and brought me limitations." A Christian has no limitations, because Christ has none, the Bishop told us. A Christian can do anything he wants to, but generally he doesn't WANT to do anything which would dishonor his commitment to God.

In a manner of speaking, a Christian should determine that he will lose all his feathers when he comes to Christ, because "old things are passed away; behold all things are become new," II Corinthians 5:17. Paul wrote to the Galations, "I live by the faith of the Son of God, who loved me and gave himself for me."

The Bishop reminded us that we will be defeated Christians if we try to live by sight, and by material things. Those of us who are saved, are told to live by faith, not by sight; by the Spirit and not by flesh. When we come to Christ, his indwelling spirit convicts us of how many old feathers we have.

We each know our own hindering feathers. Perhaps we have anger, perhaps malice or selfishness, maybe criticism or gossip or some other dirty old feather hanging onto us. We come to Him, and the Holy Spirit will put His finger on the feather, and we must be willing to throw it off.

After we have eliminated all the old feathers that have been holding us from receiving God's blessings, then we wait on God. We cannot wait on God and ask for new feathers when we still have all our old dirty ones!

The Bishop said, "That is why the eagles have better sense than we do. The eagles don't pray, "Lord, these four feathers are getting old. I want to lose only these four feathers, Lord, because the others still look good to me. So please let me lose four old ones and you give me new ones." But we Christians tend to pray that way, don't we?

The eagle says, "Why don't I make a clean breast of the whole thing and become a new creation?" In the same way, we should say, "I am going to give up all my old feathers." If we lose only four feathers, we may fly a little better, but not as well as we should, because the old ones are still hanging on.

This is one reason that Christian people are gloomy and defeated. They get tired with every little step. Why don't they let new strength come to them? Because they don't want to lose those old feathers!

The Bishop told us he did not believe in having a miserable old age. He said elderly people in India live graciously into their declining years. They are surrounded by their families, revered and blessed because of the wisdom which they pass along to the next generation. Some of us in the Western world expect to be alone and sick in our declining years. When we get flat on our backs we go to bed and say, "Praise the Lord; the Lord put me here. This is my cross to bear."

The Bishop said that people who claim their illnesses were given to them as a cross to bear are mistaken. "The Lord never gave you such a cross," he declared. "Our cross in this world is to bear witness to Jesus Christ: a cross of joy and peace."

It is not the fault of God that we suffer, because when Jesus was wounded it was for all our sin and sicknesses. These were all laid on Him; therefore, he said, don't say "It is my cross to bear!" Also, don't bring in Paul's thorn in the flesh, he told us, because Paul was not referring to sickness in that famous passage; Western people just think he did! [Look in your concordance for "thorns" and you will find that in each reference it was PEOPLE who were like thorns in the flesh, not sickness.]

The Bishop said that we should either quit calling ourselves Christians or else start practicing our faith. We shouldn't carry on as negative, defeated Christians, for this brings disgrace on the church of God. Let us try to think right, for "as a man thinketh in his heart, so is he," (Proverbs 23:7.) We can't change that law, so we must be careful what we think.

The Bishop challenged us at this point in his teaching to become a new creature, getting rid of all those old negative feathers on the spot. He encouraged us to respond to the claims of Christ. In this way we would lose all the old sinful feathers, and God could give us new ones. These new ones are love, joy, peace, long-suffering, gentleness, goodness, faith, meekness and temperance. "Now you can live like a monarch, a prince, an heir and joint-heir with Christ," he said.

He told us that he believed in healing; that every Christian ought to believe in it. "You can't believe one part of the Bible and just forget the rest of it," he said. "We have to believe all or none. We must shake off our old feathers of unbelief and live. We are saved to live! The eagles don't tell God they are poor and weak, and that there is no harm in having old feathers. Some people say, "After all, God created my feathers, and that's just my cross to bear. Lord, just let me suffer with it." No, he said, the eagles don't pray that way. This is the way that humans tend to pray, the Bishop said. Eagles have better sense; that is why they are called heavenly eagles. They know that the only way to get rid of the old feathers is to abandon themselves.

"Abandon yourself to the Lord Jesus Christ and He will give you all new feathers, beloved friends," he concluded.

Chapter 20

HOW TO DIE WELL

"The Eastern people really know how to die," the Bishop started his teaching one day. I was poised as usual with my note-taking materials, and I remember thinking, "Now, what?" I didn't have long to wait to find out what he meant.

"They have an elaborate ritual which includes calling all members of the family together to state their last wishes, to give blessings to various children, and perhaps prophesy over them." Someone said, "But how do they know when they are going to die? Wouldn't it be embarrassing to say your good-byes and then keep on living?"

"They just seem to know when the end is near," he said. "When they are finished with their comments to their family, they're just gone. "Remember in Genesis 49 where Jacob gathered his people around him and prophesied over each one of them? It says when he was through saying what he wanted, he 'brought his feet into the bed and died.' That is a typical scene in the Eastern family."

Little did I know that in a few short years, I would pick up the phone in the Editorial Room of the Springfield (Ohio) Sun and talk to a funeral director from nearby Fairborn. As he dictated the death notice, I kept writing and got my shock under control. Bishop Pillai, the dear, humble man from India who had taught us so much about the Bible, was dead, and it was I who took his obituary.

My husband, my daughter Dorothy and I went to the funeral home during calling hours, and were stunned to find him laid out in beautiful bishop's robes, a gold miter on his head, and his shepherd's staff beside him in the casket. We had never seen him in anything but his black suit and shirt with the white round collar.

I thought of the Bishop's teaching on having one's family gathered around the deathbed, and wondered if anyone was with him when he went to be with the Lord. The funeral director said that he had been living in a nursing home nearby. Needless to say, if I had known he was there, I would have visited him.

I thought of his teaching on the blessing which the Easterners bestow upon favored family members and wondered if anyone was there to gather around his bed and receive his last words. He had given up so much and traveled so far to teach the Orientalisms of the Bible, and I grieved to think that he may have died alone.

But the blessing came to mean a great deal in our family. After my husband entered the ministry, we visited his parents in Wisconsin. We found my father-in-law absorbed in a Bible which we had sent him, which was a welcome surprise, because until that time he seemed to have paid little or no attention to the Scriptures. We had a good visit, and as we went out the door to return home, my father-in-law raised his hand and said in a loud voice: "I give you my blessing!"

This made a good subject for a sermon, my husband realized, and when he was able, he made it a point to bless each one of our four children. We had done our best to teach them what the Bible requires, to receive the blessing of God; now my husband added his own to that before he was promoted to Heaven in 1988.

Many people are unaware that the familiar 12th chapter of Ecclesiastes which begins, "Remember now thy Creator in the days of thy youth..." is full of figures of speech relating to old age and dying.

[Please see *Light Through an Eastern Window* for a full explanation of what may be to many an obscure passage, available through Amazon.com.]

EPILOGUE

Teaching is a twice-blessed ministry. I have found myself first being blessed in preparing material to teach, and then experiencing gratification upon seeing others come to a new understanding of the Scriptures.

My husband used to say that when we find ourselves drawn to a certain occupation or activity, we must consider the possibility that God is calling us to that as a vocation. This is the way he felt when, as a middle-aged scientist at Wright-Patterson Air Force Base, he felt drawn to the pastorate. He resigned his position, attended seminary, and served in churches until health concerns forced him into an early retirement in 1982.

Perhaps this is the reason that he supported and encouraged my writing for Bishop Pillai. He saw the value of Christians growing in their understanding of the Bible, and he believed that spiritual growth could result from studying these Eastern Customs. It certainly is true in my case. Aside from salvation itself, my experiences in writing and teaching the Bishop's material has been my most life-changing experience.

First, it has given me an understanding of the Bible that I never imagined was possible. It has been such a blessing to really understand some of the most difficult and obscure verses in Scripture which others have puzzled over and for which they could find no explanation in available references.

But it was not enough to understand it myself; I have been further blessed by sharing the Eastern Customs with other Christians. What a thrill it has been to see their faces light up when they heard something they had not understood before.

I have met many good people who accepted the Bishop's teaching gratefully and went away blessed. I have also occasionally encountered students who are sure at the outset that they already knew everything about the Bible. If they stay in my class long enough to hear the teachings, they soon calm down and learn something in spite of themselves.

There was one lady who had read that Paul didn't permit women to teach. Upon learning that I was to be the teacher, she got up to leave, saying she could not permit herself to be disobedient to what she felt were Biblical principles.

"You know my husband is a minister," I said. "Before I left the house, he prayed for me and gave me his blessing." I could tell she was thinking it over so I started teaching and she also sat down and learned something in spite of herself.

I must say that there is a downside. Many sermons have been spoiled for me by incorrect interpretations of Scripture. I can't count the times I have heard the Samaritan woman being labeled a sinner, and Rahab the innkeeper called a prostitute. Since so many have not heard the Bishop's teaching on these matters, I just grin and bear it and pray for them to be enlightened.

Christmas is the most difficult time for me, because so many Christmas programs contain material gathered from Western traditions, sentimental hymns, and compromises for the sake of convenience in staging. For instance, I am tired of versions of the Bible which state that Mary was an unwed mother, when a little research would reveal that arranged marriages would preclude that possibility.

Where did anyone get the idea that when Jesus was born, Mary and Joseph were so poor that they dressed him in rags? Many Bible dictionaries have information on swaddling. I cringe when I see magazine articles saying the shepherds were dirty, disreputable men plying a "despised" trade, when the Scripture plainly says that shepherds were honorable men. I sigh when I see nativity scenes that include the wise men, when the Bible is quite clear that they came later to a house in Bethlehem when Jesus was a young child.

Millions in money and countless hours are spent on Christmas concerts and pageants which do not conclude with an invitation to audience members to accept Christ as their personal Savior. It is reliably reported that there are fewer conversions during the Christmas season than at any other time of year. Each Christmas season I grieve over this and think, "This should not be!" A person doesn't have to know the Eastern Customs to avoid these errors.

Well, I suppose in my lifetime I couldn't fix everything that I think ought to be fixed. In the year of our Lord 2008 I am 82 years old, and find myself pleasantly surprised that I have lived longer than I ever imagined possible.

I have been widowed twice now, and managed to survive. I approach Year 83 with faith and optimism. My four children and their families celebrate with me, as I rejoice in the goodness of God and give praise to Him for His blessings.

APPENDIX A

EASTERN CUSTOMS OF THE BIBLE

Popular Sayings
Thorn in the flesh: II Cor. 12:7, Numbers 33:55, Joshua 23:13
Samaritan woman left her waterpot, John 4:28
Heap coals of fire on his head, Romans 12:20
Servants look to the hands of their masters, Psalm 123:2
Put thy tears in my bottle, Psalm 56:8; Luke 7:44
The righteous shall flourish like the palm tree, Psa. 92:12
If the salt has lost its savor, Matt. 5:13; Seasoned with salt,
Colossians 4;6, Covenant of salt,   Numbers 18:19
When he had dipped the sop, John 13:26
It is hard for thee to kick against the pricks, Acts 26:14
He took him by the right hand, Acts 3:7
Thou are wholly gone up to the housetops? Isaiah 22:1
I will make thee as a signet, Haggai 2:23
Decree of death sealed with king's ring, Esther 3:12
No man may reverse a sealed order, Esther 8:8
Evidence sealed, Jeremiah 32:10; books sealed, Dan. 12:9
Made the sepulcher sure, sealing the stone, Matt. 27:66
Sealed with Holy Spirit, Eph 1:13, II Cor. 1:22, Eph 4:30

People of Bible times were affected by many customs, sayings, and superstitions which are not part of our culture. By becoming familiar with these, we can understand the Bible better.

APPENDIX B

CURSING AND BLESSING - AN ABSTRACT CONCEPT

Blessing or cursing – an abstract concept which can have far-reaching consequences.

1.   Advanced Manual *Speaking to Inform" -6 to 8 minutes. What does the word "Raca" mean? Matthew 5:22 - "whoever says to his brother, Raca, shall be in danger of the council".

2.   Romans 12:7 - people are instructed to bless and not curse.

3.   People who believe in curses are in bondage (voodoo priests keep the Haitians scared.)

4.   People who believe in blessings: the Hebrew people, told in their Holy Book that they are the chosen of God, that the Messiah will come from them, and all nations will be blessed. That they have survived as a people nation through the ages would be proof of this blessing. Also that the nation of Israel was re-established in 1948 is a fulfillment of prophecy found in their book.

5.   Spitting at somebody can be a curse or a blessing, depending on who does it. John 9:6 - Jesus took some dust and mixed it with spittle, and anointed the eyes of the blind man -- they thought that the spit of a holy man had magical powers.